Black Comedy

A Farce

Peter Shaffer

A SAMUEL FRENCH ACTING EDITION

SAMUEL FRENCH
FOUNDED 1830

SAMUELFRENCH.COM
SAMUELFRENCH-LONDON.CO.UK

FOR PRODUCTION ENQUIRIES

UNITED STATES AND CANADA
Info@SamuelFrench.com
1-866-598-8449

UNITED KINGDOM AND EUROPE
Plays@SamuelFrench-London.co.uk
020-7255-4302/01

Each title is subject to availability from Samuel French, depending upon country of performance. Please be aware that *BLACK COMEDY* may not be licensed by Samuel French in your territory. Professional and amateur producers should contact the nearest Samuel French office or licensing partner to verify availability.

MUSIC USE NOTE

Licensees are solely responsible for obtaining formal written permission from copyright owners to use copyrighted music in the performance of this play and are strongly cautioned to do so. If no such permission is obtained by the licensee, then the licensee must use only original music that the licensee owns and controls. Licensees are solely responsible and liable for all music clearances and shall indemnify the copyright owners of the play(s) and their licensing agent, Samuel French, against any costs, expenses, losses and liabilities arising from the use of music by licensees. Please contact the appropriate music licensing authority in your territory for the rights to any incidental music.

IMPORTANT BILLING AND CREDIT REQUIREMENTS

If you have obtained performance rights to this title, please refer to your licensing agreement for important billing and credit requirements.

BLACK COMEDY

First presented by the National Theatre at Chichester on 27th July 1965, and subsequently at the Old Vic Theatre, London, with the following cast:

Brindsley Miller	Derek Jacobi
Carol Melkett	Louise Purnell
Miss Furnival	Doris Hare
Colonel Melkett	Graham Crowden
Harold Gorringe	Albert Finney
Schuppanzigh	Paul Curran
Clea	Maggie Smith
Georg Bamberger	Michael Byrne

Directed by John Dexter
Setting by Alan Tagg

This revised version first performed in September 1993 by the Roundabout Theatre Company, New York.

CHARACTERS

Brindsley Miller, a young sculptor (mid-twenties), intelligent and attractive, but nervous and uncertain of himself.

Carol Melkett, Brindsley's fiancée. A young débutante; very pretty, very spoiled; very silly. Her sound is that unmistakable, terrifying débutante quack.

Miss Furnival, a middle-aged lady. Prissy and refined. Clad in the blouse and sack skirt of her gentility, her hair in a bun, her voice in a bun, she reveals only the repressed gestures of the middle-class spinster— until alcohol undoes her.

Colonel Melkett, Carol's commanding father. Brisk, barky, yet given to sudden vocal calms which suggest a deep and alarming instability. It is not only the constant darkness which gives him his look of wide-eyed suspicion.

Harold Gorringe, the bachelor owner of an antique-china shop, and Brindsley's neighbour, Harold comes from the North of England. His friendship is highly conditional and possessive: sooner or later, payment for it will be asked. A specialist in emotional blackmail, he can become hysterical when slighted, or (as inevitably happens) rejected. He is older than Brindsley by several years.

Schuppanzigh, a German refugee, chubby, cultivated, and effervescent. He is an entirely happy man, delighted to be in England, even if it means being employed full time by the London Electricity Board.

Clea, Brindsley's ex-mistress. Mid-twenties; dazzling, emotional, bright and mischievous. The challenge to her to create a dramatic situation out of the darkness is ultimately irresistible.

Georg Bamberger, an elderly millionaire art collector, easily identifiable as such. Like Schuppanzigh, he is a German.

The action of the play takes place in Brindsley's apartment in South Kensington, London

Time: 9.30 on a Sunday night in the mid Sixties

In memory
of Jerry Weinstein
who laughed

and to
John Dexter
who helped so much
to make the laughter

BLACK COMEDY

Brindsley's apartment in South Kensington, London. This forms the ground floor of a large house now divided into flats. Harold Gorringe lives opposite; Miss Furnival lives above

There are four ways out of the room. A door UL leads directly across the passage to Harold's room. The door to this, with its mat laid tidily outside, can clearly be seen. A curtain UC screens Brindsley's studio: when it is parted we glimpse samples of his work in metal. To the right of this, an open stair shoots steeply up to his bedroom above, reached through a door at the top. A trap in the floor DL leads down to the cellar

It is a room, when we finally see it, full of colour and space and new shapes. It is littered with objects—mobiles, manikins, toys, and dotty bric-à-brac—the happy paraphernalia of a free and imaginative mind. The total effect is of chaos tidied in honour of an occasion, and of a temporary elegance created by the furniture borrowed from Harold and arranged to its best advantage. This consists of three elegant Regency chairs in gold leaf, a Regency chaise-longue to match, a small Queen Anne table bearing a fine opaline lamp with a silk shade, a Wedgwood bowl, a good Coalport vase containing summer flowers, and a fine porcelain Buddha

The only things which actually belong to Brindsley are a cheap square table bearing the drinks; an equally cheap round table in the middle of the room, shrouded by a cloth and decorated with the Wedgwood bowl; a low stool DC, improved by the Buddha; a record player; and his own artistic creations. These are largely assumed to be in the studio awaiting inspection; but one of them is visible in this room. On the dais stands a bizarre iron sculpture dominated by two long detachable metal prongs, and hung with metal pieces which jangle loudly if touched. On the wall hang paintings, some of them presumably by Clea. All are non-figurative: colourful geometric designs, splashes, splodges, and splats of colour; whirls and whorls and wiggles—all testifying more to a delight in handling paint than to an ability to achieve very much with it

Complete darkness

NB: On the few occasions when a lighter is lit, matches are struck, or a torch is put on, the light on stage merely gets dimmer. When these objects are extinguished, the stage immediately grows brighter

Two voices are heard: Brindsley and Carol. They must give the impression of two people walking round a room with absolute confidence, as if in the light. We hear sounds as of furniture being moved. A chair is dumped down

Brindsley (*exhausted*) There! How do you think the room looks?

Pause

Carol (*quacking*) Fabulous! I told you it would. I wish you could always have it like this. That lamp looks divine there. And those chairs are just the right colour. I told you green would look well in here.
Brindsley Suppose Harold comes back?
Carol He is not coming back till tomorrow morning.

We hear Brindsley pacing nervously

Brindsley I know. But suppose he comes tonight? He's mad about his antiques. What do you think he'll say if he goes into his room and finds out we've stolen them?
Carol Don't dramatize. We haven't stolen *all* his furniture. Just … (*slowly*) two chairs, the sofa, the table, the lamp, the bowl and the vase of flowers, that's all.
Brindsley And the Buddha. That's more valuable than anything.
Carol Oh, do stop worrying, darling.
Brindsley Well, you don't know Harold. He won't even let anyone *touch* his antiques.
Carol Look, we'll put everything back as soon as Mr Bamberger leaves. Now stop being dreary.
Brindsley Well, frankly, I don't think we should have done it. I mean— *anyway*, Harold or no.
Carol Why not, for heaven's sake? The room looks divine now. Just *look* at it!

Tiny pause

Brindsley Darling, George Bamberger's a multi-millionaire. He's lived his life against this sort of furniture. Our few stolen bits aren't going to impress him. He's coming to see the work of an unknown sculptor. If you ask me, it would look much better to him if he found me exactly as I really am: a poor artist. It might touch his heart.

Carol It might—but it certainly won't impress Daddy. Remember, he's coming too.

Brindsley As if I could forget! Why you had to invite your monster father tonight, I can't think!

Carol Oh, not again!

Brindsley Well, it's too bloody much. If he's going to be persuaded I'm a fit husband for you, just by watching a famous collector buy some of my work, he doesn't deserve to have me as a son-in-law!

Carol He just wants some proof you can earn your own living.

Brindsley And what if Bamberger *doesn't* like my work?

Carol He will, darling. Just stop worrying.

Brindsley I can't... Get me a whisky.

She does: we hear her steps, and a glass clink against a bottle—then the sound of a the soda syphon

(*Grimly*) I've got a foreboding. It's all going to be a disaster. An A-one, copper-bottomed, twenty-four-carat disaster!

Carol The trouble with you is you're what Daddy calls a "D.D."—a Determined Defeatist.

Brindsley The more I hear about your Daddy, the more I hate him. I loathe military men, anyway... And in any case, he's bound to hate *me*.

Carol Look, darling, all you've got to do is stand up to him. Daddy's only a bully when he thinks people are afraid of him.

Brindsley Well, I am.

Carol You haven't even met him.

Brindsley That doesn't make any difference. I'm a complete physical coward. He'll smell it on my breath.

Carol Don't be ridiculous. (*She hands him a drink*) Here.

Brindsley Thanks.

Carol What can he do to you?

Brindsley For one thing, he can refuse to let me marry you.

Carol Ah, that's sweetipoo.

We hear them embrace

Brindsley I like you in green. It goes with your hair.
Carol Straighten your tie. You look sloppypoo.
Brindsley Well, you look divine.
Carol Really?
Brindsley I mean it. I've never seen you look so lovely.
Carol Tell me, Brin, have there been many before me?
Brindsley Thousands.
Carol Seriously.
Brindsley Seriously—none.
Carol What about that girl in the photo?
Brindsley She lasted about three months.
Carol When?
Brindsley Two years ago.
Carol What was her name?
Brindsley Clea.
Carol What was she like?
Brindsley She was a painter. Very honest. Very clever. And just about as cosy as a steel razor-blade.
Carol When was the last time you saw her?
Brindsley (*evasively*) I told you ... two years ago.
Carol Well, why did you still have her photograph in your bedroom drawer?
Brindsley It was just there, that's all. Give me a kiss...

Pause

No-one in the world kisses like you.
Carol (*murmuring*) Tell me something... Did you like it better with her— or me?
Brindsley Like what?
Carol Sexipoo.
Brindsley Look, people will be here in a minute. Put a record on. It had better be something for your father. What does he like?
Carol (*crossing to the record player*) He doesn't like anything except military marches.
Brindsley I might have guessed... Wait—I think I've got some! That last record on the shelf. The orange cover. It's called *Marching and Murdering with Sousa*, or something.
Carol This one?

Brindsley That's it.
Carol (*getting it*) *The Band of the Coldstream Guards.*
Brindsley Ideal. Put it on.
Carol How d'you switch on?
Brindsley The last knob on the left. That's it... Be sure to plug it in. Let
us pray! (*Distinctly*) Oh God, let this evening go all right! Let Mr
Bamberger like my sculpture and buy some! Let Carol's monster father
like *me*! And let my neighbour Harold Gorringe never find out that we
borrowed his precious furniture behind his back! Amen.

*A Sousa march; loud. Hardly has it begun, however, when it runs down—
as if there is a failure of electricity. The sound stops*

*Brilliant Light floods the stage. The rest of the play, save for the times
when matches are struck, or a flashlight is switched on, is acted in this
light, but as if in pitch darkness*

*They freeze: Carol by the end of the sofa; Brindsley by the drinks table. The
girl's dress is a silk flag of chic wrapped round her greyhound's body. The
boy's look is equally cool: narrow, contained, and sexy. Throughout the
evening, as things slide into disaster for him, his crisp, detached shape
degenerates progressively into sweat and rumple—just as the elegance of
his room gives way relentlessly to its usual near-slum appearance. For the
place, as for its owner, the evening is a progress through disintegration*

Oh, blast! We've blown a fuse! (*He blunders to the light switch,
gingerly feeling ahead of him, trying to part the darkness with his
hands. Finding the switch, he flicks it on and off*) The record-player
must have caused it. We need another fuse.
Carol Where's the box?
Brindsley In the hall.
Carol Have you any candles?
Brindsley I don't think so.
Carol (*testily*) Well, where are the matches?
Brindsley They should be on the drinks table. (*He feels round the bottles*)
No... Try on that bloody player.

They both start groping about the room, feeling for matches

Carol Nothing here.

Brindsley Damn, damn, damn, damn, damn, damn!

The telephone rings

Would you believe it?! (*He blunders his way towards the sound of the bell. Just in time he remembers the central table—and stops himself colliding into it with a smile of self-congratulation*) All right: I'm coming! (*Instead he trips over the dais, and goes sprawling—knocking the phone on to the floor. He has to grope for it on his knees, hauling the receiver back to him by the wire. Into the receiver*) Hallo? ... (*In sudden horror*) Hallo! ... No, no, no, no—I'm fine, just fine! ... You? ... (*His hand over the receiver; to Carol, coolly*) Darling—look in the bedroom, will you?

Carol I haven't finished in here yet.

Brindsley Well, I've just remembered there are some fuses in the bedroom. In that drawer where you found the photograph. Go and get one, will you?

Carol I don't think there are. I didn't see any there.

Brindsley (*snapping*) Don't argue. Just look!

Carol All right. Keep your hairpiece on. (*During the following she gropes her way cautiously up the stairs—head down, arms up the banisters, silken bottom thrust out with the effort*)

Brindsley (*controlling himself*) I'm sorry. I'm sure there are some there. You must have missed them.

Carol What about the matches?

Brindsley We'll have to mend it in the dark, that's all. Please hurry, darling.

Carol (*climbing*) Oh God, how dreary...

Brindsley (*listening to hear Carol go, then into the phone*) Hallo? ... Well, well, well, well! How are you? Good. That's just fine. Fine, fine! ... Stop saying what?

Carol reaches the top of the stairs—and from force of habit pulls down her skirt before groping her way into the bedroom

(*Hand still over the receiver; calling up*) Carol? ... Darling? ... (*Satisfied she has gone; in a rush into the telephone, his voice low*) Clea! What are you doing here? I thought you were in Finland... But you've hardly been gone six weeks... Where are you speaking from? The air terminal? ... Well, no—that's not a good idea tonight. I'm terribly busy, and I'm afraid I just can't get out of it. It's business.

Carol (*calling from the bedroom, above*) There's nothing here except your dreary socks. I told you.

Brindsley (*calling back*) Well, try the other drawers! (*He rises as he speaks, turning so that the wire wraps itself around his legs*)

Carol returns to her search

(*Low and rapid, into the phone*) Look: I can't talk now. Can I call you tomorrow? Where will you be? ... Look, I told you *no*, Clea. Not tonight. I know it's just around the corner, that's not the point. You can't come round... Look the situation's changed... Something's happened this past month——

Carol (*off*) I can't see anything. Brin, *please!*

Brindsley Clea, I've got to go! ... Look, I can't discuss it over the phone... Has it got to do with *what?* Yes, of course it has. I mean, you can't expect things to stay frozen, can you?

Carol emerges from the bedroom

Carol There's nothing here. Haven't we any matches at all?

Brindsley Oh, stop wailing! (*Into the phone*) No, not you! I'll call you tomorrow. Goodbye. (*He hangs up sharply but fails to find the rest of the telephone, so that he bangs the receiver hard on the table first. Then he has to disentangle himself from the wire. Already he is beginning to be fussed*)

Carol (*descending*) Who was that?

Brindsley Just a chum. Did you find the fuse?

Carol I can't find anything in this. We've *got* to get some matches!

Brindsley I'll try the pub.

Little screams are heard approaching from above. It is Miss Furnival groping her way downstairs in a panic

Miss Furnival (*off; squealing*) Help! Help...! Oh, please, someone help me...!

Brindsley (*calling out*) Is that you, Miss Furnival?

Miss Furnival (*off*) Mr Miller...?

Brindsley Yes?
Miss Furnival (*off*) Mr Miller!
Brindsley Yes!

Miss Furnival gropes her way in

Brindsley crosses to find her, but narrowly misses her

Miss Furnival Oh, thank God, you're there; I'm so frightened!
Brindsley Why? Have your lights gone too?
Miss Furnival Yes!
Brindsley It could be a black-out. (*He finds her hand and leads her to the chair* DL)
Miss Furnival I don't think so. The street lights are on in the front. I saw them from the landing.
Brindsley (*in despair*) Then it must be the master fuse box. It controls the whole house!
Carol Well, where is that?

Miss Furnival gasps at the strange voice

Brindsley Down in the cellar. It's all sealed up. No-one's allowed to touch it but the electricity people. They have to come round and repair it themselves! It's under the floor over there. (*He points to the trap door*)
Carol (*imperiously*) Well, you have to get them. Quick!
Brindsley How?
Carol Phone them, of course. Don't be so futile.
Brindsley But they won't come at this time of night.
Carol Don't be such a D.D., darling! *Try!*

Brindsley accidentally touches Miss Furnival's breast. She gives a little scream. Brindsley gropes his way to the phone

Brindsley Have you by any chance got a match on you, Miss Furnival?
Miss Furnival I'm afraid I haven't. So improvident of me. And I'm absolutely terrified of the dark!
Brindsley Darling, this is Miss Furnival, from upstairs. Miss Furnival— Miss Melkett.
Miss Furnival How do you do?

Carol (*extending her hand by habit, in the dark*) How do you do?
Miss Furnival Isn't this frightful?

Brindsley picks up the phone and dials "O"

Brindsley Perhaps we can put Mr Bamberger off.
Carol Didn't you say he's dining out and coming on here after.
Brindsley Yes.
Carol So he can't be reached.
Brindsley Oh, *hell!* (*He sits on the dais and speaks into the phone*) Hallo, Operator. The London Electricity Board, please. Night Service. (*He pauses*) I'm sure it's in the book, Miss, but I'm afraid I can't see... There's no need to apologize. No, I'm not blind—I just can't see! ... We've got a fuse... (*Exasperated*) No, we *haven't* got any matches! (*Desperate*) Miss, *please*: this is an emergency! ... Thank you! (*To the room*) London is staffed with imbeciles!
Miss Furnival Oh, you're so right, Mr Miller.
Brindsley (*rising, frantic; into the phone*) Miss, I *don't want* the number: I can't dial it! ... Well, have *you* ever tried to dial a number in the dark? (*Trying to keep control*) I just want to be connected... Thank you. (*To Miss Furnival*) Miss Furnival, do you by any remote chance have any candles?
Miss Furnival I'm afraid not, Mr Miller.
Brindsley (*mouthing nastily at her*) "I'm afraid not, Mr Miller." (*Briskly, into the phone*) Hallo? Look, I'd like to report a main fuse at 18 Scarlatti Gardens. My name is Miller. (*Exasperated*) Yes, yes! All right...! (*Maddened; to the room*) Hold on! Hold bloody on...!
Miss Furnival If I might suggest, Harold Gorringe opposite might have some candles. He's away for the weekend, but always leaves his key under the mat.
Brindsley What a good idea! That's just the sort of practical thing he would have! (*To Carol*) Here—take this... I'll go and see. (*He hands her the telephone in a fumble—then makes for the door—only to collide with his sculpture*) Bugger!
Miss Furnival Are you all right, Mr Miller?
Brindsley I knew it! I bloody knew it. This is going to be the worst night of my life...! (*He collides with the door*)

Brindsley stumbles out, and is seen groping under Harold's mat for the key. He finds it and enters the room opposite

Carol (*into the phone*) Hallo? Hallo? (*To Miss Furnival*) This would have
to happen tonight. It's just Brindsley's luck.

Miss Furnival Is it something special tonight then, Miss Melkett?

Carol It couldn't be more special if it tried.

Miss Furnival Oh dear. May I ask why?

Carol Have you ever heard of a German called George Bamberger?

Miss Furnival Indeed, yes. Isn't he the richest man in the world?

Carol Yes. (*Into the phone, impatiently*) Hallo...? (*To Miss Furnival*)
Well, he's coming here tonight.

Miss Furnival Tonight!

Carol In about twenty minutes, to be exact. And to make matters worse,
he's apparently *stone deaf*!

Miss Furnival How extraordinary...! May I ask why he's coming?

Carol He saw some photos of Brindsley's work and apparently got madly
excited about it. He's a great collector. Brin would be absolutely *made*
if Bamberger bought a piece of his.

Miss Furnival Oh, how exciting!

Carol It's his big break. Or was—till a moment ago.

Miss Furnival Oh, my dear, you *must* get some help. Jiggle that thing.

Carol (*jiggling the phone*) Hallo? Hallo...? Perhaps the Bomb's fallen,
and everyone's dead.

Miss Furnival Oh, please don't say things like that—even in levity.

Carol (*someone answers her at last*) Hallo? Ah! This is Number 18,
Scarlatti Gardens. I'm afraid we've had the most dreary fuse. It's what's
laughingly known as the master box. We want a *little man*! ... Well, they
can't *all* have flu... Oh, please try! It's screamingly urgent... Thank
you. (*She hangs up*) Sometime this evening, they hope. That's a lot of
help!

Miss Furnival They're not here to help, my dear. In my young days you
paid for service and you got satisfaction. Nowadays you just get some
foreigner swearing at you. And if they think you're of the middle class,
that only makes it worse.

Carol Would you like a drink?

Miss Furnival I don't drink, thank you. My dear father, being a Baptist
minister, strongly disapproved of alcohol.

A scuffle is heard among milk bottles off, followed by a stifled oath

Colonel (*off*) Damn and blast!! (*Barking*) Is there anybody there?

Carol (*calling*) In here, Daddypoo.
Colonel (*off*) Can't you put the light on, dammit? I've almost knocked meself out on a damn milk bottle.
Carol We've got a fuse. Nothing's working.

Colonel Melkett appears, holding a lighter which evidently is working—we can see the flame, and, of course, the lights go down a little

Miss Furnival Oh, what a relief! A light!
Carol This is my father, Colonel Melkett—Miss Furnival. She's from upstairs.
Colonel (*shortly*) Good evening!
Miss Furnival I'm taking refuge for a moment with Mr Miller. I'm not very good in the dark.
Colonel When did this happen?

Miss Furnival, glad for the light, follows it pathetically as the Colonel crosses the room

Carol Five minutes ago. The main thingy just went.
Colonel And where's this young man of yours?
Carol In the flat opposite. He's trying to find candles.
Colonel You mean he hasn't got any?
Carol No. We can't even find the matches.
Colonel I see. N.O. No Organization. Bad sign!
Carol Daddy, please. It could happen to any of us.
Colonel Not to me. (*He turns to find Miss Furnival right behind him and glares at her balefully*)

The poor woman retreats to the sofa and sits down. Colonel Melkett gets his first sight of Brindsley's sculpture

What the hell's that?
Carol Some of Brindsley's work.
Colonel Is it, by Jove? And how much does that cost?
Carol I think he's asking fifty pounds for it.
Colonel My God!
Carol (*nervously*) Do you like the flat, Daddy? He's furnished it very well, hasn't he? I mean it's rich, but not gaudipoo.

Colonel (*mining a chair*) Very elegant—good: I can see he's got
  proper taste. (*He sees the Buddha*) Ah, now that's what I understand by
  a real work of art—you can see what it's meant to be.
Miss Furnival Good heavens!
Carol What is it?
Miss Furnival Nothing ... it's just that Buddha—it so closely resembles
  the one Harold Gorringe has.

Carol looks panic-stricken

Colonel It must have cost a pretty penny, what? He must be quite well
  off... By Jove—it's got pretty colours! (*He bends to examine it*)
Carol (sotto voce, *urgently, to Miss Furnival*) Do you *know* Mr Gorringe?
Miss Furnival Oh, very well indeed! We're excellent friends. He has
  such lovely things... (*For the first time she notices the sofa on which she
  is sitting*) Oh...!
Carol What?
Miss Furnival This furniture... Surely...? (*She looks about her realiz-
  ing*) Oh, my goodness!
Carol (*hastily*) Daddy, why don't you look in there? It's Brin's studio.
  There's something I particularly want you to see before he comes back.
  Please have a look...
Colonel Very well, Dumpling. Anythin' to oblige. (*To Miss Furnival*)
  Excuse me.

Colonel goes off into the studio, taking his lighter with him

*The Light instantly gets brighter on stage. Carol sits beside the spinster
on the sofa, crouching like a conspirator*

Carol (*low and urgent*) Miss Furnival, you're a sport, aren't you?
Miss Furnival I don't know. What is this furniture doing in here? It
  belongs to Harold Gorringe.
Carol I know. We've done something absolutely frightful. We've stolen
  all his best pieces and put Brin's horrid old bits in *his* room.
Miss Furnival But why? It's disgraceful!
Carol (*sentimentally*) Because Brindsley's got nothing, Miss Furnival.
  Nothing at all. He's as poor as a church mouse. If Daddy had seen this
  place as it looks normally, he'd have forbidden our marriage on the spot.
  Mr Gorringe wasn't there to ask—so we just took the chance.

Miss Furnival If Harold Gorringe knew that anyone had touched his
furniture or his porcelain, he'd go out of his mind! And as for that
Buddha—(*she points in the wrong direction*) it's the most precious
piece he owns. It's worth hundreds of pounds.

Carol Oh, please, Miss Furnival—you won't give us away, will you?
We're desperate! And it's only for an hour... Oh, please! *Please!*

Miss Furnival (*giggling*) Very well...! I won't betray you!

Carol Oh, thank you!

Miss Furnival But it'll have to go back exactly as it was, just as soon as
Mr Bamberger and your father leave.

Carol I swear! Oh, Miss Furnival, you're an angel! Do have a drink. Oh,
no, you don't. Well, have a bitter lemon.

Miss Furnival Thank you. That I won't refuse.

The Colonel returns, still holding his lighter. The stage darkens a little

Colonel And that's supposed to be sculpture?

Carol (*coldly*) It's not supposed to be. It is.

Colonel They'd make good garden implements. I'd like 'em for turnin'
the soil.

Miss Furnival giggles

Carol That's not very funny, Daddy.

Miss Furnival stops giggling

Colonel Sorry, Dumpling. Speak as you find.

Carol I wish you wouldn't call me Dumpling.

Colonel Well, there's no point wastin' this. We may need it! (*He snaps
off his lighter*)

Miss Furnival gives her little gasp as the stage brightens

Carol Don't be nervous, Miss Furnival. Brin will be here in a minute with
the candles.

Miss Furnival Then I'll leave, of course. I don't want to be in your way.

Carol You're not at all. (*She hears Brindsley*) Brin?

Brindsley comes out of Harold's room—returns the key under the mat

Brindsley Hallo?
Carol Did you find anything?
Brindsley (*coming in*) You can't find anything in this! If there's candles there, *I* don't know where they are. Did you get the electric people?
Carol They said they might send someone around later.
Brindsley How much later?
Carol They don't know.
Brindsley That's a lot of help. What a lookout! Not a bloody candle in the house. A deaf millionaire to show sculpture to—and your monster father to keep happy. Lovely!
Colonel (*grimly lighting his lighter*) Good evenin'.

The stage darkens. Brindsley jumps

Carol Brin, this *is* my father—Colonel Melkett.
Brindsley (*wildly embarrassed*) Well, well, well, well, well...! (*He panics*) Good evening, sir. Fancy you being there all the time! I—I'm expecting some monsters—neighbours—some neighbour monsters, monster neighbours, you know... They rang up and said they might look round... Well, well, well...!
Colonel You seem to be in a spot of trouble.
Brindsley (*with mad nervousness*) Oh, not really! Just a fuse—nothing really, we have them all the time... I mean, it won't be the first fuse I've survived, and I dare say it won't be the last! (*He gives a wild braying laugh*)
Colonel (*relentless*) In the meantime, you got no matches, right?
Brindsley Right.
Colonel No candles, right?
Brindsley Right.
Colonel No B.E., right?
Brindsley B.E.?
Colonel Basic Efficiency.
Brindsley I wouldn't say that, exactly...
Colonel By that I mean the simple state of being *At Attention* in life...
Brindsley A.A. At Attention. Sorry.
Colonel ...rather than At Ease.
Brindsley Well, I'm certainly not at ease.
Colonel So, what are you going to do about it?
Brindsley Do?
Colonel Don't echo me, sir. I don't like it.

Brindsley You don't like it... I'm sorry.

Colonel Now look you here. This is an emergency. Anyone can see that.

Brindsley No-one can see anything: that's the emergency! (*He gives his nervous laugh*)

Colonel Spare me your humour, sir, if you don't mind. Let's look at the situation objectively. Right?

Brindsley Right.

Colonel Good. Problem... (*He snaps off the lighter*)

The Lights brighten

...darkness. Solution—light!

Brindsley Oh very good, sir.

Colonel Weapons: matches—candles—torches! Anything else?

Brindsley A set of early Christians.

Colonel What did you say?

Brindsley Nothing, sir. Matches, candles, torches, very good.

Colonel (*fiercely*) Well, where might you find all or any of those, at this time of night?

Brindsley I haven't the faintest idea.

Colonel The pub, of course! You have a pub close by, haven't you?

Brindsley (*babbling*) Oh yes, I spend all my time there! Well some of my time. A little of my time. Ten minutes a day at the most...

Colonel It won't be closed yet, if you hurry.

Brindsley Thank you, sir. Your clarity of mind has saved the day!

Colonel Well, get on with it, man.

Brindsley Yes, sir! Yes sir! Back in a minute!

The Colonel sits in the Regency chair, DR

Carol Good luck, darling.

Brindsley Thank you, my sweet.

She blows him a kiss. He blows her one back

Colonel (*irritated*) Stop that at once!

Brindsley starts for the door, but as he reaches it, Harold Gorringe is heard, off stage. He speaks with a broad Lancashire accent

Harold (*off*) Hallo? Hallo? Anyone there?
Brindsley (*freezing with horror*) Harold!!
Harold (*off*) Brindsley!
Brindsley (*meant for Carol*) It's Harold! He's back!
Carol Oh no!
Brindsley *The furniture!!*
Harold (*off*) What's going on here?

*Harold appears. He wears a smart raincoat, over a tight, modish, grey
suit and a brilliant strawberry shirt, and carries a small weekend bag
with handles. His hair falls over his brow in a flossy attempt at elegance*

Brindsley Nothing, Harold.
Harold Brindsley!
Brindsley Don't go in there—come in here! We've had a fuse. It's dark—
it's all over the house.
Harold Have you phoned the electric people?
Brindsley (*reaching out and grabbing him*) Yes. Come in here.
Harold (*grabbed*) Ohh…! (*He takes Brindsley's hand and enters the
room on his arm*) It's rather cosy in the dark, isn't it?
Brindsley (*desperately*) Yes! I suppose so… So, you're back from your
weekend then…
Harold I certainly am, dear. Weekend! Some weekend! I couldn't take
it any more. It rained the whole bloody time. I feel damp to my panties.
Brindsley (*nervously*) Well, have a drink and tell us all about it.
Harold Us? (*Disengaging himself*) Who's here, then?
Miss Furnival (*archly*) I am, Mr Gorringe.
Harold Ferny?
Miss Furnival Taking refuge, I'm afraid. You know how I hate the dark.
Colonel (*attempting to light his lighter*) Blasted thing! It's beginning to
go. (*He succeeds with the lighter*)

The stage darkens

There we are! (*Raising the lighter to Harold's face, with distaste*) Who
are *you*?
Brindsley May I present my neighbour. This is Harold Gorringe—
Colonel Melkett.
Harold How do?
Colonel (*coldly*) How d'ye do?

Brindsley And this is Carol Melkett, Harold Gorringe.
Carol (*giving him a chilly smile*) Hallo...!?

Harold nods coldly

Brindsley Here, let me take your cape, Harold.
Harold (*taking it off and handing it to him*) Be careful, it's sopping wet.

Adroitly, Brindsley drops the raincoat over the Wedgwood bowl on the table

Colonel You've got no candles, I suppose?
Harold Would you believe it, Colonel, but I haven't! Silly me!

Brindsley crosses and blows out the Colonel's lighter, just as Harold begins to look around the room. The stage brightens

Colonel What the devil did you do that for?
Brindsley I'm saving your wick, Colonel. You may need it later and it's failing fast.

The Colonel gives him a suspicious look. Brindsley moves quickly back, takes up the coat and drops it over the right end of the sofa, to conceal as much of it as possible

Harold It's all right. I've got some matches.
Carol (*alarmed*) Matches!
Harold Here we are! I hope I've got the right end. (*He strikes one*)

The stage darkens. Brindsley immediately blows it out from behind—the stage lightens—then moves swiftly to hide the Wedgwood bowl under the table and drop the tablecloth over the remaining end of the sofa. Miss Furnival sits serenely unknowing between the two covers

Hey, what was that?
Brindsley (*babbling*) A draught. No match can ever stay alight in this room. It's impossible. Cross currents...
Harold (*bewildered*) I don't know what you're talking about. (*He strikes another match*)

The stage darkens. Brindsley again blows it out—the stage brightens—as he nips over to sit in the chair DL, but this time is seen

(*Irritated*) What's up with you?
Brindsley Nothing!
Harold Have you got a dead body in here or something?
Brindsley Of course not. It's just that it's dangerous! (*He improvises frantically*) Deeply dangerous…! We can all die in this room, actually.
Harold Die?

Brindsley clutches Harold and backs him bewilderedly across to the centre table

Brindsley Yes—I've just remembered…! It's something they always warn you about! In old houses the master fuse box and the gas line are close together. They are down there!
Colonel So what about it?
Brindsley Well … electrical blowouts can damage the gas supply. They're famous for it! They do it all the time! And they say you've got to avoid all naked flames till they're mended.
Colonel (*suspiciously*) I've never heard of that.
Harold Me neither.
Brindsley Oh, it's absolutely true. It's fantastically dangerous to burn naked flames in this room! Isn't it, Carol?
Carol (*catching on*) Oh—yes! Brin's absolutely right! In fact, they warned me about it on the phone this evening when I called them. They said, "Whatever you do, don't strike a match till the fuse is mended". It's dreadfully—*dreadfully*—dangerous. You can't *imagine* how dreadfully!
Brindsley There, you see!
Colonel (*grimly*) Then why didn't you warn me, Dumpling?
Carol I—I forgot.
Colonel Brilliant!
Miss Furnival Oh, goodness, we must take care!
Brindsley We certainly must…!

Pause

Let's all have a drink. Cheer us up…!
Harold Well, I must say, that wouldn't come amiss. Not after the journey

I've had tonight. I swear to God there was thirty-five people in that compartment if there was one—babes in arms, toddlers, two nuns, three yapping poodles, and not a sausage to eat from Leamington to London. It's a bloody disgrace. Excuse me. I'll just go and clean up first.

Brindsley (*panicking*) You can do that here!

Harold Well, I must unpack anyway.

Brindsley Do it later.

Harold No, I hate to keep clothes in a suitcase longer than I absolutely have to. If there's one thing I can't stand, it's a creased suit.

Brindsley Nonsense, Harold. We can't have you walking about in the dark. You'll knock yourself unconscious—you know how accident-prone you are. You just stay in here with us, and relax. (*To Carol*) Darling, pour Harold a drink for God's sake.

Harold (*pleased*) Well, you're in a bossy mood, I must say. Darkness must bring out the dominant in you! (*He sits on the sofa, putting his bag on the floor*)

Carol What will you have, Mr Gorringe? Winnie, Vera, or Ginette?

Harold Come again?

Carol Winnie Whisky, Vera Vodka, or dear old standby Ginette.

Harold (*yielding*) Well, I can see you're a camp one...! If it's all the same to you, I'll have a drop of Ginette, please, and a little lime juice.

Colonel (*irritated*) Young man, do I have to keep reminding you that you are in an emergency? You have a guest arrivin' any second.

Brindsley Oh, God, I'd forgotten!

Colonel Try the pub. Try the neighbour's. Try who you damn well please, sir—but *get some light.*

Brindsley Yes ... yes...! (*Airily*) Carol, can I have a word with you, please?

Carol I'm here. (*She gropes toward him*)

Brindsley leads her to the stairs

Colonel *What now?!*

Brindsley Excuse us just a moment, please, Colonel. (*He pulls her quickly after him up the stairs*)

Miss Furnival (*as Brindsley and Carol go up the stairs*) Oh, Mr Gorringe, it's so exciting. You'll never guess who's coming here tonight.

Harold Who...?

Miss Furnival Guess.

Harold The Queen.

Miss Furnival Oh—you are ridiculous...

Brindsley arrives at the top of the stairs, then opens the bedroom door and closes it behind Carol and himself. We hear them talk from behind the door

Brindsley (*frantically*) What are we going to *do*!?
Carol I don't know.
Brindsley Think!
Carol I can't. The whole thing's a nightmare.
Colonel Is that boy touched or what?
Harold Touched? He's a lollipop.
Colonel A what?
Harold An absolute sweetie. I've known him since he came here. There's not many secrets we keep from each other, I can tell you.
Colonel (*frostily*) Really?
Brindsley I'll have to put all Harold's furniture back in his room right now!
Carol In the dark?
Brindsley There's no other way. I can't get lights till we do!
Harold Well, come on, Ferny: don't be a tease. Who is it who's coming here?
Miss Furnival I'll give you a clue. It's someone with money.
Harold Money...? Let me think...!
Colonel (*calling*) Carol?
Carol Look, can you just tell him it was a joke?
Brindsley You don't know him. He can't bear anyone to touch his treasures. It's bad enough in his china shop. The things he keeps at home are absolutely *sacred*. Do you want him to call me a thief in front of your father? Because that's exactly what he'll do.
Colonel (*a little louder*) Brindsley!
Brindsley I'm not exaggerating. He can get absolutely murderous when he's upset. He turns into a mad killer inside ten seconds!
Carol Well, how on earth can we do it? You can't get all that stuff out in the dark—then put your own things back in here without anyone knowing. It's impossible!
Brindsley Now who's being a D.D.?
Colonel (*louder*) Brindsley...! What are you two doin' up there?
Harold It's no good, Colonel. You can't hear a thing up in that bedroom.
Brindsley (*stripping off his jacket*) Listen now. You hold the fort. Serve

them drinks. Keep things going, and leave everything else to me. I can get it all back—every piece!

Carol You can't...! It's impossible...!

Colonel (*roaring*) Brindsley!!

Brindsley (*dashing to the door*) Coming, sir...! (*Opening it, with a false calm*) I'm just getting some empty bottles to take back to the pub.

Colonel Say what you like, that boy is touched.

Brindsley (*to Carol; intimately*) Trust me, darling. Just trust me... You do your part—I'll do mine.

They kiss

Colonel (*bellowing*) Get down here, Miller!

Brindsley Yes, sir! Yes, sir! (*He rushes out and in his anxiety he misses his footing and falls neatly down the entire flight of stairs. He picks himself up, trying for calm*) I'm off now, Colonel! Help is definitely on the way.

Colonel And hurry it up, man.

Carol follows downstairs

Brindsley Carol will give you drinks. If our guest arrives, just explain the situation to him.

Harold (*feeling for his hand*) Would you like me to come with you?

Brindsley (*breaking free*) No, no, no—good heavens: stay and dry out those wet clothes. A nice gin and lime will do wonders for you. I shan't be a minute everyone... Bye! (*He reaches the door, opens it, then slams it loudly, remaining on the inside. Stealthily he opens it again, stands dead still for a moment,* C, *silently indicating to himself the position of the chairs he has to move—quickly removes his shoes, puts them under the drinks table—then finds his way to the first of the Regency chairs* DL, *which he lifts noiselessly*)

Carol (*with bright desperation*) Well now, drinks! It's Ginette for Mr Gorringe and I suppose Winnie for Daddy. And I'll have a nice glass of Vera and tonic.

Colonel And how on earth are you going to do all that in the dark?

Carol I remember the exact way I put out the bottles.

Brindsley bumps into her with the chair and falls back, gored by its leg

It's very simple.

Harold Oh, look, luv, let me strike a match. I'm sure it's not that dangerous, just for a *minute*! (*He strikes a match*)

The stage darkens

Carol Oh, no!

Brindsley ducks down, chair in hand, and Carol blows out the match. The stage brightens

Do you want to blow us all up, Mr Gorringe...? All poor Mr Bamberger would find would be teensy-weensy bits of us. Very messipoo! (*She snatches the box of matches, feels for the ice bucket, and drops them into it*)

As Carol, fumbling, starts to mix drinks, Brindsley steals out, Felix-the-cat-like, with the chair. He sets it down, opens Harold's door, and disappears inside it with the chair

Harold Bamberger? Is that who's coming? George Bamberger?
Miss Furnival Yes. To see Mr Miller's work. Isn't it exciting?
Harold Of course: money! Well, I never! I read an article about him last week in the Sunday paper. He's known as the mystery millionaire. He's almost completely deaf—deaf as a post—and spends most of his time indoors alone with his collection. He hardly ever goes out, except to a gallery or a private studio. That's the life! If I had money that's what I'd do. Just collect all the china and porcelain I wanted.

Brindsley returns with a poor, broken-down chair of his own and sets it down in the same position as the one he has taken out. The second chair presents a harder challenge. It sits right across the room, UR. Delicately, Brindsley moves toward it—but he has difficulty finding it. We watch him walk around and around it in desperately narrowing circles till he touches it and with relief picks it up

Miss Furnival I've never met a millionaire. I've always wondered if they feel different to us. I mean their actual skins.
Colonel Their skins?

Miss Furnival Yes. I've always imagined they must be softer than ours. Like the skins of ladies when I was a girl.

Carol What an interesting idea.

Harold Oh, she's very fanciful is Ferny. Real imagination. I always say, she could have been a writer.

Miss Furnival Very kind of you, Mr Gorringe. You're always so generous with your compliments.

During the following exchange between Miss Furnival and Harold, Brindsley moves the second Regency chair across what should be Miss Furnival's field of vision, two inches from her face. Brindsley unfortunately misaims and carries the chair past the door, bumps into the wall, retreats from it, and inadvertently shuts the door softly with his back. Now he cannot get out of the room. He has to set down the chair, grope desperately for the door handle—try to find it, turn it, then open the door—then refind the chair, which he has quite lost. This takes a long and frantic time. At last he triumphs, and staggers from the room nearly exhausted

(*Staring smugly into the darkness, hands clasped in maidenly gentility*) But this is by no means fancy. In my day, softness of skin was quite the sign of refinement. Nowadays, of course, it's hard enough for us middle classes to keep ourselves decently clothed, let alone soft.

Harold You never spoke a truer word, Ferny. It's all going to the dogs—everywhere you look. Take that word you've just used—"refinement". That doesn't mean anything any more. People used it once to indicate something gracious—something elegant and old-world. Not any more. If you were to say "refinement" to most people today, they'd think it was something to do with sugar.

Brindsley returns with an old rocking-chair of his own. He starts to cross gingerly to where the Colonel is sitting, feeling his way with one hand extended before him. Halfway across he entangles his feet in the handles of Harold's bag, and drags it after him. He staggers about wildly, holding the rocking-chair and trying to free his feet from the handles. Finally he succeeds

NB: If the counterpoint of Brindsley's farce action goes well, Harold and Miss Furnival may have to ad lib a little during it, and not mind if the

*audience cannot hear them. The essential thing for all four actors during
the furniture-moving is to preserve the look of ordinary conversation*

Miss Furnival That is the tragedy of our times, Mr Gorringe. And such
a charming word, too. (*She savours it*) "Refinement!"
Harold I'll tell you the truth, dear. You and I are never going to hear that
word spoken properly again in our lifetime—because no-one gives a
damn any more. They haven't got a clue, and they don't give a damn.
And you and I have simply got to get used to it.
Miss Furnival You know, my father used to say, even before the bombs
came and burned our dear little house at Wendover: "The game's up, my
girl. We middle classes are as dead as the dodo." Poor Father, how right
he was.
Colonel Your father was a professional man?
Miss Furnival He was a man of God, Colonel.
Colonel Ah.

*Brindsley sets the rocking-chair down immediately next to the Colonel's
chair*

How are those drinks comin', Dumpling?
Carol Fine, Daddy. They'll be one minute.
Colonel (*speaking directly into Brindsley's face*) Let me help you.

Brindsley pulls back, startled

Carol You can take this bitter lemon to Miss Furnival if you want.
Colonel Very well.

*Colonel rises just as Brindsley's hand pulls the chair from beneath him.
With his other hand Brindsley pulls the rocker into the identical position.
The Colonel moves slowly across the room, arms outstretched for the
bitter lemon. Unknowingly, Brindsley follows him, carrying the third
chair. The Colonel collides gently with the table. At the same moment
Brindsley reaches it upstage of him, and searches for the Wedgwood bowl.
Their hands narrowly miss. Then Brindsley remembers the bowl is under
the table. Deftly, he reaches down and retrieves it*

*Carrying the bowl in one hand and the chair in the other, Brindsley
triumphantly leaves the room through the arch unconsciously provided*

by the outstretched arms of Carol and the Colonel, giving and receiving
a glass of scotch—which they think is bitter lemon

Carol Here you are, Daddy. Bitter lemon for Miss Furnival.
Colonel Right you are, Dumpling. (*To Miss Furnival*) So your father was
a minister, then?
Miss Furnival He was a saint, Colonel. I'm only thankful he never lived
to see the rudeness and vulgarity of life today.

The Colonel sets off to find her but goes much too far to the right

Harold (*sitting on the sofa beside her*) Oooh, you're so right, Ferny.
Rudeness and vulgarity—that's it to a T. The manners of some people
today are beyond belief. Honestly. Did I tell you what happened in my
china shop last Friday? I don't think I did.
Miss Furnival No, Mr Gorringe, I don't think so.

Her voice corrects the Colonel's direction. During the following he moves
slowly up toward her from behind

Harold Well, I'd just opened up—it was about quarter to ten and I was
dusting off the teapots—you know, Wedgwood collects the dust something shocking!—when who should walk in but that Mrs Levitt, you
know—the ginger-haired bit I told you about, the one who thinks she's
God's gift to bachelors.
Colonel (*finding Miss Furnival's head with his hand and presenting her*
with the scotch) Here's your bitter lemon.
Miss Furnival Oh, thank you. Most kind. (*Throughout Harold's story,*
Miss Furnival nurses the glass, not drinking)

The Colonel finds his way slowly back to the chair he thinks he was sitting
on before, but which is now a rocker

Brindsley reappears, triumphantly carrying one of the original Re-
gency chairs he took out. He sets it down—feels its back and sides—
realizes his mistake—and escapes with it out of the room again

Harold Anyway, she's got in her hand a vase I'd sold her last week—it
was a birthday present for an old geezer she's having a bit of a ding-dong
with somewhere in Earl's Court, hoping to collect all his loot when he

dies, as I read the situation. I'm a pretty good judge of character, Ferny, as you know—and she's a real grasper if ever I saw one.

The Colonel sits heavily in the rocking-chair which overbalances backwards, spilling him on to the floor

Colonel Dammit to hell!
Carol What's the matter, Daddy?

A pause. The Colonel feels the rocking-chair and sets it on its feet

Colonel (*unbelieving*) It's a blasted rockin' chair! I didn't see a blasted rockin' chair here before! (*Astounded, he stays on the floor*)

Brindsley re-appears with a second cheap old chair of his own. He sets it down where the second Regency chair he moved had been

Harold Oh yes, dear, you want to watch that. It's in a pretty ropey condition. I've told Brin about it several times. Anyway, this vase. It's a nice bit of Kang Tsi porcelain, blue and white, absolutely authentic— I'd let her have it for sixty pounds, and she'd got infinitely the best of the bargain, no arguments about that! (*He rises and leans against the centre table to tell his story more effectively*)

The Colonel seats himself again, gingerly, in the rocking chair

Well, in she prances, her hair all done up in one of them bouffant hairdos, you know, tarty—French-like—it would have looked fancy on a girl half her age with twice her looks——

Brindsley mistakenly lifts the end of the sofa. Miss Furnival gives a gasp at the jolt

Exactly! You know the sort.

Brindsley staggers in the opposite direction down stage on to the rostrum

And d'you know what she says to me? "Mr Gorringe," she says, "I've been cheated."
Miss Furnival No!

Harold "I took this vase over to Bill Everett in the Portobello market, and he says it's not what you called it at all, Chinese and very rare. He says it's a piece of twentieth century trash from Taiwan!"

Brindsley finds the lamp on the downstage table and picks it up. He walks with it around the rocking chair, on which the Colonel is now sitting again

"Does he?" I say. "Does he?" I keep calm. I always do when I'm riled. "Yes," she says. "He does. And I'd thank you to give me my money back!"

The wire of the lamp has followed Brindsley around the bottom of the rocking chair. It catches. Brindsley tugs it gently. The chair moves. Surprised, the Colonel is jerked forward. Brindsley tugs it again, much harder. The rocking chair is pulled over forward, spilling the Colonel out of it, again on to the floor, and then falling itself on top of him. The shade of the lamp comes off. During the ensuing dialogue, Brindsley gets to his knees and crawls right across the room following the flex of the lamp. He finds the plug, pulls it out and—still on his knees—retraces his steps, winding up the wire around his arm, and becoming helplessly entangled in it. The Colonel remains on the floor, now really alarmed

Miss Furnival How dreadful, Mr Gorringe. What did you do?
Harold I counted to ten, and then I let her have it. "In the first place," I said, "I don't expect my customers to go checking up on my honesty behind my back. In the second, Bill Everett is as ignorant as Barnsley dirt; he doesn't know Ming from Ping. And in the third place, that applies to you, too, Mrs Levitt. Don't you ever cross my threshold, because, if you do, I won't make myself responsible for the consequences."
Carol (*with two drinks in her hand*) My, Mr Gorringe, how splendid of you. Here's your gin and lime. You deserve it. (*She hands him the bitter lemon*)
Harold (*accepting it*) I was proper blazing, I didn't care!
Carol Where are you? Where are you, Daddy? Here's your scotch.
Colonel Here, Dumpling! (*He gets up dazedly and fumbles his way to the glass of gin and lime*)

Brindsley meanwhile realizes he has lost the shade of the lamp. On his knees, he begins to look for it

Harold Carroty old bitch—telling me about pottery! (*He shakes himself indignantly at the recollection of it*)
Miss Furnival Do you care for porcelain yourself, Colonel?
Colonel I'm afraid I don't know very much about it, madam. I like some of that Chinese stuff—you get some lovely colours, like on that statue I saw when I came in here—very delicate.
Harold What statue's that, Colonel?
Colonel The one on the packing case, sir. Very fine.
Harold I didn't know Brin possessed any Chinese stuff. What's it of then, this statue?

Brindsley freezes

Carol (*desperately*) Well, we've all got drinks, I'd like to propose Daddy's regimental toast. Raise your glasses everyone! "To the Twenty-fifth Horse. Confusion to its enemies!"
Miss Furnival I'll drink to that! *Confusion!*
Harold Up the old Twenty-fifth!!

Quickly, Brindsley finds the Buddha, moves it from the packing case to the table, then gets Harold's raincoat from the sofa, and wraps the statue up in it, leaving it on the table

Colonel Thank you, Dumpling. That was very touchin' of you. Very touchin' indeed. (*He swallows his drink*) Dammit, that's gin!
Harold (*drinking*) I've got bitter lemon!
Miss Furnival Oh! Horrible...! Quite horrible! That would be alcohol, I suppose...! Oh dear, how unpleasant...! (*Seizing her chance, she downs a huge draft of scotch*)
Harold (*to Miss Furnival*) Here, luv, exchange with me. No—you get the bitter lemon—but I get the gin. Colonel——
Colonel Here, sir. Scotch for me.

They all exchange drinks. Brindsley resumes his frantic search for the shade

Harold Here, Ferny.

The Colonel hands her the gin and lime. He gets instead the bitter lemon from Harold. Harold gets the scotch

Miss Furnival Thank you.
Harold Well, let's try again. Bottoms up!
Colonel Quite.

They drink. Triumphantly, Brindsley finds the shade. Unfortunately, as he marches toward the Colonel on his knees, the Colonel spits out his bitter lemon in a fury all over him

Look here—I can't stand another minute of this! (*He fishes his lighter out of his pocket and angrily tries to light it*)
Carol Daddypoo, please!
Colonel I don't care, Dumpling. If I blow us up, then I'll blow us up! This is ridiculous...! (*He lights the lighter*)

The lighting dims

(*He stares at where the Buddha had been when he last saw it. He examines the empty space*) There was a Buddha sitting there when I came in. Where is it now?
Harold A Buddha? What kind of Buddha? I didn't know Brindsley had a Buddha?
Brindsley (*blurting it out in panic*) I don't! I wouldn't have a Buddha in the house! I'm a Confucian. (*He claps his hands over his mouth*)

All of them look at him—on his knees, all wound round with lamp wire by the table. Pause

Colonel What the devil are you doin' there?
Brindsley Now don't be rash, Colonel. No naked flames, remember? (*He blows out the lighter*)

The stage brightens

Colonel Don't be impertinent! Did you go to the pub?
Brindsley Certainly. But it was closed.
Harold You didn't go to the pub in that time, surely? You couldn't have.
Brindsley Of course I did.
Miss Furnival But it's five streets away, Mr Miller.
Brindsley Needs must when the Devil drives, Miss Furnival. Whatever the hell that means.

Quickly, Brindsley lifts the table, and steals out of the room with it and the wrecked lamp

Colonel (*thinking Brindsley is still kneeling at his feet*) Now look here: there's somethin' very peculiar goin' on in this room. I may not know about art, Miller, but I know men. I know a liar in the light, and I know one in the dark.
Carol Daddypoo!
Colonel I don't want to doubt your word, sir. All the same, I'd like your oath you went out to that public house. Well?
Carol (*realizing he isn't there, raising her voice*) Brin, Daddy's talking to you!
Colonel What are you shouting for?

Brindsley rushes back from Harold's room, still entangled in the lamp

Brindsley Of course! I know! He's absolutely right.
Colonel Well? What's your answer?
Brindsley That was a very perceptive remark you made there, sir. Not everyone would have thought of that.
Colonel Now look you here. I've been extremely patient with you, young man. But enough is enough. It's P.E. now—Patience Exhausted. If you think I'm going to let my daughter marry a born liar, you are very much mistaken.
Carol Daddy—please!
Colonel Quiet, Dumpling. Let me handle this.
Brindsley What's there to handle, sir, for heaven's sake?
Harold *Marry!* Did he say *marry*?
Carol Well, that's the general idea.
Harold You and this young lady, Brin?
Carol Are what's laughingly known as engaged. Subject of course to Daddy's approval.
Harold Well, I never! (*Furious at the news and at the fact that Brindsley hasn't confided in him*) What a surprise.
Brindsley We were keeping it a secret.
Harold Evidently. How long's this been going on, then?
Brindsley A few months.
Harold You sly cat.
Brindsley (*nervously*) I hope you approve, Harold.

Harold You sly, secretive cat. You certainly know how to keep things to yourself, don't you?

Brindsley I meant to tell you, Harold. You were the one person I was going to tell...

Harold But you didn't.

Brindsley I—I—I never got around to it.

Harold You chose to keep it from me.

Brindsley I didn't choose—I just forgot.

Harold Say no more. There's no obligation to share confidences. I've only been your neighbour for three years. I've always assumed there was more than a geographic closeness between us, but I was obviously mistaken.

Brindsley Oh don't start getting huffy, Harold!

Harold I'm not getting anything. It'll just teach me not to bank on so-called friendship. It's silly me again! Silly, stupid, trusting me!

Colonel Good God, man!

Miss Furnival rises in agitation and gropes her way to the drinks table

Carol (*wheedling*) Now come, Mr Gorringe. We haven't told anybody. Not one single soulipoo. Really.

Colonel At the moment, Dumpling, there's nothing to tell. And I'm not sure there's going to be!

Brindsley Look, sir, we seem to have got off on the wrong foot. If it's my fault, I apologize.

Miss Furnival (*groping about on the drinks table*) My father always used to say, "To err is human: to forgive divine."

Carol I thought that was somebody else.

Miss Furnival (*blithely*) So many people copied him. (*She finds the open bottle of gin, lifts it and sniffs it eagerly*)

Carol May I help you, Miss Furnival?

Miss Furnival No, thank you, Miss Melkett. I'm just getting myself another bitter lemon. That is—if I may, Mr Miller?

Brindsley Of course. Help yourself.

Miss Furnival Thank you, most kind! (*She pours more gin into her glass and returns slowly to sit up stage on the edge of the rostrum*)

Colonel Well, sir, wherever you are——

Brindsley Here, Colonel.

Colonel I'll overlook your damn peculiar behaviour this once, but understand this, Miller. My daughter's dear to me. You show me you can look after her, and I'll consider the whole thing favourably. I can't say fairer than that, can I?

Brindsley No, sir. Most fair, sir. Most fair. (*He pulls a hideous face one inch from the Colonel's*)

Carol Of course he can look after me, Daddy. His works are going to be world-famous. In five years I'll feel just like Mrs Michelangelo.

Harold (*loftily*) There wasn't a Mrs Michelangelo, actually.

Carol (*irritated*) Wasn't there?

Harold No. He had passionate feelings of a rather different nature.

Carol Really, Mr Gorringe. I didn't know that.

Brindsley Look, Harold, I'm sorry if I've hurt your feelings. Can't we all be friends?

Harold I'm not sure that I can contemplate a friendly relationship with a viper.

Clea enters, wearing dark glasses and carrying a flight bag. She stands in the doorway, amazed by the dark. She takes off her glasses, but this doesn't improve matters. It still remains dark for her. She puts them on again, then off in perplexity

Carol (*winningly*) Come on, Mr Gorringe. It really is a case of forgive and forgettipoo. Have another Ginette and lime. (*She rises and mixes the drink*)

Harold (*rising*) Oh, all right. I don't mind if I do.

Carol Let me mix it for you.

Clea crosses the room to the sofa. Harold crosses to Carol, narrowly missing Clea, and gets his drink

Harold Well, I must say there's nothing nicer than having a booze-up with a pretty girl.

Carol (*archly*) You haven't seen me yet.

Harold Oh, I just know it. Brindsley always had wonderful taste. I've often said to him, you've got the same taste in ladies as I have in porcelain.

Harold and Brindsley—one from up stage, one from across the room— begin to converge on the sofa. On the word "modest" all three, Clea in the middle, sit on it. Brindsley of course imagines he is sitting next to Harold

Brindsley Harold!

Carol Oh, don't be silly, Brin. Why be so modest? There's nothing to be ashamed about, if anything, it's rather flattering. I found a photograph of one of his bits from two years ago, and I must say she was pretty stunning, in a blowsy sort of way.

Harold Which one was that, then? I suppose she means Clea.

Clea reacts

Carol Did you know her, Mr Gorringe?

Harold Oh yes. She's been around a long time.

Brindsley nudges Clea warningly—imagining she is Harold. Clea gently bumps against Harold

Carol (*surprised*) Has she?

Harold Oh yes, dear. Or am I speaking out of turn?

Brindsley Not at all. I've told Carol all *about* Clea. (*He bangs Clea again, a little harder*)

Clea correspondingly bumps against Harold

Though I must say, Harold, I'm surprised you call three months "a long time".

Clea shoots him a look of total outrage at this lie. Harold is also astonished

Carol What was she like?

Brindsley (*meaningfully, into Clea's ear*) I suppose you can hardly remember her, Harold.

Harold (*speaking across her*) Why on earth shouldn't I?

Brindsley Well, since it was two years ago, you've probably forgotten.

Harold Two years?!

Brindsley *Two years ago!* (*He punches Clea so hard that the rebound knocks Harold off the sofa, drink and all*)

Harold (*picking himself up; spitefully*) Well, now since you mention it, I remember her perfectly. I mean, she's not one you can easily forget!

Carol Was she pretty?

Harold No, not at all. In fact, I'd say the opposite. Actually she was rather plain.

Brindsley She wasn't!

Harold I'm just giving my opinion.

Brindsley You've never given it before.

Harold (*leaning over Clea*) I was never *asked*! But since it's come up, I always thought she was ugly. For one thing, she had teeth like a picket fence—yellow and spiky. And for another, she had bad skin.

Brindsley She had nothing of the kind!

Harold She did. I remember it perfectly. It was like a new pink wallpaper, with an old grey crumbly paper underneath.

Brindsley This is disgraceful.

Harold You knew I never liked her, Brindsley. She was too clever by half.

Miss Furnival And so tiresomely Bohemian.

Carol You mean she was as pretentious as her name?

Clea, who has been reacting to this last exchange of comments about her like a spectator at a tennis match, now reacts to Carol open-mouthed

I bet she was. That photograph I found showed her in a sort of sultry peasant blouse. She looked like *The Bartered Bride* done by Lloyds Bank Operatic Society.

They laugh, Brindsley hardest of all. Guided by the noise, Clea aims her hand and slaps his face

Brindsley Ahh!

Carol What's wrong?

Miss Furnival What is it, Mr Miller?

Brindsley (*furiously*) That's not very funny, Harold. What the hell's the matter with you?

Clea makes her escape. Brindsley rises

Harold (*indignantly*) With me?

Brindsley Well, I'm sure it wasn't the Colonel.

Colonel What wasn't, sir?

Brindsley, groping about, catches Clea by the bottom, and instantly recognizes it

Brindsley *Clea!* (*In horror*) Clea!

*Clea breaks loose and moves away from him. During the following, he
tries to find her in the dark, and she narrowly avoids him: reaching the
table, she picks up a bottle of scotch, and rejects it in favour of vodka,
which she takes with her*

Colonel What?
Brindsley I was just remembering her, sir. You're all talking the most
    awful nonsense. She was beautiful... And anyway, Harold, you just said
    I was famous for my taste in women.
Harold Ay, but it had its lapses.
Brindsley (*frantically moving about*) Rubbish! She was beautiful and
    tender and considerate and kind and loyal and witty and adorable in
    every way!
Carol You told me she was as cosy as a steel razor-blade.
Brindsley Did I? Surely not! It doesn't sound like me.
Carol You said to me in this room when I asked you what she was like,
    "She was a painter. Very honest. Very clever, and just about as cosy—"
Brindsley (*stopping, exasperated*) As a steel razor-blade! Well then, I
    said it! So bloody what...?
Carol So nothing!

*He throws out his hands in a gesture of desperate exhaustion and bumps
straight into Clea. They instantly embrace, Clea twining herself around
him, her vodka bottle held aloft. A tiny pause*

Colonel If that boy isn't touched, I don't know the meaning of the word!
Carol What's all this talk about her being kind and tender, all of a sudden?
Brindsley (*tenderly, holding Clea*) She could be. On occasion. *Very.*
Carol Very rare occasions, I imagine.
Brindsley Not so rare. (*He kisses Clea again*) Not so rare at all. (*He leads
    Clea softly past the irritated Carol, toward the stairs*)
Carol Meaning what, exactly...? (*She shouts*) Brindsley I'm talking to
    you!!
Brindsley (*sotto voce, into Clea's ear as they stand just behind Harold*)
    I can explain. Go up to the bedroom. Wait for me there.
Harold (*in amazement: thinking he is being addressed*) Now? Do you
    think this is quite the moment?
Brindsley Oh, God...! I wasn't talking to you!
Carol What did you say?

Harold (*to Carol*) I think he wants *you* upstairs. (*Slyly*) For what purpose,
I can't begin to imagine.
Colonel They're going to do some more of that plotting, I dare say.

*Carol joins the other two on the stairs. We see all three groping blindly up
to the bedroom, Brindsley's hands on Clea's hips, Carol's hands on
Brindsley's hips*

Carol (*with a conspirator's stage whisper*) What is it, darling? Has
something gone wrong?

The following dialogue is spoken sotto voce *on the stairs*

Brindsley It's all back—every bit of it.
Carol You mean, we can have lights?
Brindsley Yes... *No!!*
Carol Why not?
Brindsley Never mind!
Carol Why do you want me in the bedroom?
Brindsley I don't! Go away!
Carol Charming!
Brindsley I didn't mean that.
Colonel There you are. They *are* plotting again. (*He calls up*) What the
hell is going on up there?
Brindsley Nothing, Colonel. I've just remembered—there may be a torch
under my bed. I keep it to blind the burglars with. Have another drink,
Colonel! (*He puts Clea into the bedroom and shuts the door behind
them*)
Colonel What d'you mean another? I haven't had *one* yet!
Miss Furnival Oh! Poor Colonel! Let me get you one.
Colonel (*rising*) I can get one for myself, thank you. Let me get you
another bitter lemon.
Miss Furnival (*rising*) No, thank you, Colonel, I'll manage myself.

*They grope toward the drinks table. Above, Clea and Brindsley sit on the
bed*

Clea So this is what they mean by a blind date! What the hell is going on?
Brindsley (*sarcastically*) Nothing! George Bamberger is only coming to
see my work tonight, and we've got a main fuse.

Clea Is that the reason for all this furtive clutching?
Brindsley Look, I can't explain things at the moment.
Clea Who's that—(*débutante accent*) "frightful gel"?
Brindsley Just a friend.
Clea She sounded more than that.
Brindsley Well, if you must know, it's Carol. I've told you about her.
Clea The Idiot Deb?
Brindsley She's a very sweet girl. As a matter of fact we've become very
  good friends in the last six weeks.
Clea How good?
Brindsley Just good.
Clea And have you become friends with her father too?
Brindsley If it's any of your business, they've just dropped in to meet Mr
  Bamberger.
Clea What was it you wanted to tell me on the phone tonight?
Brindsley Nothing.
Clea You're lying!
Brindsley Look, Clea, if you ever loved me, just slip away quietly with
  no more questions, and I'll come round later and explain everything, I
  promise.
Clea I don't believe you.
Brindsley Please, darling … please … please … please!

They kiss, passionately, stretched out on the bed

Colonel (*pouring*) At last … a decent glass of scotch. Are you getting your
  bitter lemon?
Miss Furnival (*cheerfully pouring herself an enormous gin*) Oh yes,
  thank you, Colonel!
Colonel I'm just wonderin' if this Bamberger fellow is goin' to show up
  at all. He's half an hour late already.
Harold Oh! That's nothing, Colonel. Millionaires are always late. It's
  their thing.
Miss Furnival I'm sure you're right, Mr Gorringe. That's how *I* imagine
  them. Hands like silk, and always two hours late.
Brindsley (*disengaging himself*) No-one in the world kisses like you.
Clea I missed you badly, Brin. I had to see you. I've thought about nothing
  else these past six weeks. Brin, I made the most awful mistake walking
  out.
Brindsley Clea—*please!*

Clea I mean we've known each other for four years. We can't just throw each other away like old newspapers.

Brindsley I don't see why not. You know my politics, you've heard my gossip, and you've certainly been through all my entertainment section.

Clea Well, how about a second edition?

Brindsley Darling, we simply can't talk about this now. Can't you trust me just for an hour?

Clea Of course I can, darling. You don't want me down there?

Brindsley No.

Clea Then I'll get undressed and go quietly to bed. When you've got rid of them all, I'll be waiting.

Brindsley That's a terrible idea!

Clea (*reaching for him*) I think it's lovely. A little happy relaxation for us both.

Brindsley (*falling off the bed*) I'm perfectly relaxed!

Carol Brindsley!

Clea "Too solemn for day, too sweet for night. Come not in darkness, come not in light." That's me, isn't it?

Brindsley Of course not. I just can't explain now, that's all.

Clea Oh, very well, you can explain later … in bed!

Brindsley Not tonight, Clea.

Clea Either that or I come down and discover your sordid secret.

Brindsley There *is* no sordid secret!

Clea Then you won't mind my coming down!

Carol
Colonel } (*roaring together*) Brindsley!!!

Brindsley Oh, God!…! All right, stay. Only keep quiet… Blackmailing bitch! (*He emerges at the top of the stairs*) Yes, my sweet?

Carol What are you doing up there? You've been an eternity!

Brindsley I… I… I'm just looking in the bathroom, my darling. You never know what you might find in that clever little cabinet!

Colonel (*moving to the stairs*) Are you trying to madden me, sir? Are you trying to put me in a fury, sir?

Brindsley Certainly not, sir!

Colonel I warn you, Miller, it's not difficult! My furies are not unknown, sir.

Clea I may sing!

Clea goes off into the bathroom

Brindsley (*to Clea*) I may knock your teeth in!
Colonel What did you say?
Carol Brin! How dare you talk to Daddy like that!
Brindsley *Oh!!* I wasn't talking to Daddy like that...
Carol Then who *were* you talking to?
Brindsley No-one! *Myself*, I was talking to myself! I was saying—"If you keep groping about up here like this, you may knock your teeth in!"
Colonel Mad...! Mad...! It's the only explanation—you've got yourself engaged to a lunatic.
Carol There's something going on up there, and I'm coming up to find out what it is. Do you hear me, Brin?
Brindsley Carol—no!
Carol (*climbing the stairs*) I'm not such a fool as you take me for. I know when you're hiding something. Your voice goes all deceitful—very, very foxypoo!

Schuppanzigh enters. He wears the overcoat and peaked cap of the London Electricity Board and carries a large toolbag, similarly labelled

Brindsley Darling, please. That's not very ladylike... I'm sure the Colonel won't approve of you entering a man's bedroom in the dark!
Carol I'm comin' up, Brindsley, I'm comin' up!!!
Brindsley (*scrambling down*) I'm coming down, Carol... I'm coming down...

Schuppanzigh speaks with a German accent

Schuppanzigh 'Allo, please? Mr Miller? Mr Miller? I've come as was arranged.
Brindsley My God ... it's Bamberger!
Carol Bamberger?
Brindsley Yes, Bamberger. (*He rushes down the remaining stairs, pulling Carol with him*)
Schuppanzigh You must have thought I was never coming! (*He takes off his overcoat*)
Brindsley (*airily*) Noo, no... Not at all! I'm delighted you could spare the time. I know how busy you are. I'm afraid we've had the most idiotic disaster. We've had a fuse.

Harold You'll have to speak up, dear, he's stone deaf!

Brindsley (*yelling*) We've had a mains fuse—not the best conditions for seeing sculpture.

Schuppanzigh Please not to worry. Here! (*He produces a torch from his pocket and "lights" it*)

The Light on stage dims a little, as usual, to indicate this. All relax with audible sighs of pleasure

Carol Oh, what a relief!

Brindsley (*hastily dragging the sheet over the rest of the sofa*) Do you always travel with a torch?

Schuppanzigh Mostly, yes. It helps to see details. (*He sees the others*) You are holding a private view?

Brindsley Oh no. These are just some friends…! (*He yells in his ear*) May I present Colonel Melkett?

Colonel (*yelling in his other ear*) A great honour, sir!

Schuppanzigh (*banging his ear, to clear it*) No, no, mine—mine!

Brindsley Miss Carol Melkett!

Carol (*screeching in his ear*) I say: hallo! So glad you got here! It's terribly kind of you to take such an interest!

Schuppanzigh Not at all.

Brindsley Harold Gorringe—a neighbour of mine!

Harold (*shouting*) How do? Very honoured, I'm sure.

Schuppanzigh Enchanted.

Harold I must say it's a real thrill, meeting you!

Brindsley And another neighbour, Miss Furnival!

Schuppanzigh Enchanted.

Miss Furnival (*hooting in his ear*) I'm afraid we've all been taking refuge from the storm, as it were. (*She takes hold of Schuppanzigh's hand*) Oh! It is true! They are softer! Much, much softer! (*She strokes his hand*)

Schuppanzigh (*utterly confused*) Softer? Please?

Brindsley and Harold pull Miss Furnival away, and she subsides on to the sofa

Brindsley Miss Furnival, please!

Schuppanzigh Excuse me, but why are you all shouting at me? I'm not deaf.

Brindsley (*to Harold*) You told me he was.

Harold I read he was.

Miss Furnival (*sadly*) My father was.
Brindsley I'm terribly sorry, sir. A misunderstanding.
Harold (*fawningly*) I love your outfit ... and where did you get that smart little cap?
Schuppanzigh My cap?
Carol Yes—it's so chic! Wildly original!
Schuppanzigh But surely you've seen them before? We all have them.
Harold You mean it's some kind of club? I bet it's very exclusive!
Schuppanzigh Oh yes! Absolutely impossible to get into...!

They all laugh

Miss Furnival (*standing up*) My father always used to say, it is easier for a rich man to go through the eye of a needle, than for a camel to enter heaven.
Harold (*warningly*, sotto voce) Ferny!

Above, Clea enters, wearing the top half of Brindsley's pyjamas and nothing else. She gets into bed, still clutching the vodka bottle and carrying a plastic toothmug

Brindsley Oh, Christ!
Carol What!
Brindsley (*sotto voce*) The sofa...! I'd forgotten about *the sofa*! Let's get that bloody torch away from him!
Schuppanzigh (*shining his torch at them*) Excuse me, but I am pressed for time.
Brindsley Of course—of course... (*He throws himself on the sofa, spreading wide his arms to conceal it*)
Schuppanzigh (*he spies the sculpture in iron*) Oh Gott in Himmel...! Is that one of yours?
Brindsley Yes.
Schuppanzigh It's amazing. Absolutely phantastisch!
Brindsley You really think so?
Schuppanzigh But definitely. I see at once what it represents.
Colonel You do?
Schuppanzigh Oh, no question. The two needles of man's unrest. Self-love and self-hate, leading to the same point! (*He swings the torch back to Brindsley*)

Brindsley again covers the sofa with his body

I'm right, aren't I?

Brindsley Absolutely... It's easy to see you're an expert, sir!

Schuppanzigh Aber nein, nein!

Miss Furnival moves unsteadily up stage, towards the sofa

Brindsley May I suggest an experiment? I would love you to feel it in the dark!

Schuppanzigh The dark?

Brindsley Yes. I actually made that piece to be felt, not seen. I call it my theory of Factual Tactility. If it doesn't stab you to the quick, it's not Art. (*To Carol*) Darling, why don't you relieve our distinguished guest of his torch, and he can try this for himself?

Schuppanzigh surrenders his torch to Carol, who turns it off. The stage brightens. Immediately, Brindsley rises from the sofa

Carol Oh yes. Of course...

Brindsley Now stretch out your arms and feel it all over, sir. With passion—that's the trick. Total *commitment!*

Schuppanzigh and drunken Miss Furnival both lift their arms. The electrician embraces the sculpture with a fervent clash. The spinster bumps gently into the sofa, and collapses on it full length

During the following speech, Brindsley stealthily pulls the sofa up stage into the studio, bearing on it the supine Miss Furnival, who waves goodbye vaguely as she disappears. Then he draws the curtain, concealing her

Schuppanzigh Ach—wunderbar! Impaled here in the dark, one can feel the vital thrust of the argument. The anguish of our times! It has real moral force! I feel the passionate embrace of similarities to create an orgasm of opposites.

Carol Oh, how super!

Schuppanzigh You should charge immense sums for work like this, Mr Miller. This one, for example, how much is this?

Brindsley Fifty——

Carol Five hundred guineas!

Schuppanzigh Ach so! (*He pauses*) Well...

Harold Would you like it then?
Schuppanzigh Very much.
Colonel (*amazed*) For five hundred guineas?
Schuppanzigh Certainly—if I had it!

All laugh fawningly

Harold You mean you've gone broke?
Schuppanzigh No. I mean I never had it.
Colonel Now look, sir, I know millionaires are supposed to be eccentric...
Carol Daddy, ssh!
Schuppanzigh Millionaires? Who do you think I am?
Colonel Dammit, man! You must know who you are!
Carol Mr Bamberger, is this some kind of joke you like to play?
Schuppanzigh Excuse me. That is not my name.
Brindsley It isn't?
Schuppanzigh No. My name is Schuppanzigh. Franz Immanuel Schuppanzigh. Born in Weimar, 1905. Student of philosophy at Heidelberg, 1934. Refugee to this country, 1938. Regular employment ever since—with the London Electricity Board!
Carol Electricity!
Brindsley You mean you're not—?
Harold Of course he's not!
Schuppanzigh But who did you imagine I was?
Harold (*furiously*) How dare you? (*He snatches the electrician's torch from Carol and turns it on*)

The stage darkens

Schuppanzigh (*retreating before him*) Please?
Harold Of all the nerve, coming in here, giving us a lecture about orgasms, and all the time you're simply here to mend a fuse!
Colonel I agree with you, sir. It's monstrous!
Schuppanzigh (*bewildered*) It is?

The Colonel snatches the torch and shines it pitilessly in the man's face

Colonel You come in here, a public servant, pretending to be deaf, and proceed to harangue your employers, unasked and uninvited.
Schuppanzigh (*bewildered*) Excuse me. But I *was* invited.

Colonel Don't answer back. In my day you would have been fired on the spot for impertinence.

Carol Daddy's absolutely right! Ever since the Beatles, the lower classes think they can behave exactly as they want.

Colonel (*handing the torch to Brindsley*) Miller, will you kindly show this feller his work?

Brindsley (*exasperated*) Why don't you just go into the cellar?

Schuppanzigh (*snatching the torch, equally exasperated*) All right! Where is it?

Harold (*seizing the torch*) I'll do it. (*To Schuppanzigh*) Come on. Down you go. Come on, get a move on!

Schuppanzigh All right! So—farewell!

Schuppanzigh descends through the trap, taking the torch with him

(*Calling up from below*) I leave the light of Art for the dark of Science!

Harold Let's have a little less of your lip, shall we? (*He slams the trapdoor down irritably after him*)

The Lights immediately come up full. There is a long pause. All stand about embarrassed. Suddenly they hear the noise of Miss Furnival singing Rock of Ages *in a high drunken voice from behind the curtain. Above, attracted by the noise of the slam Clea gets out of bed, still clutching the vodka and toothmug, opens the door, and stands at the top of the stairs listening*

Brindsley None of this evening is happening.

Carol Cheer up, darling. In a few minutes everything will be all right. Mr Bamberger will arrive in the light—he'll adore your work and give you twenty thousand pounds for your whole collection.

Brindsley (*sarcastically*) Oh, yes!

Carol Then we can buy a super little house and live what's laughingly known as happily ever after. I want to leave this place just as soon as we're *married*.

Clea hears this. Her mouth opens wide with astonishment

Brindsley (*nervously*) Shhhh!

Carol Why? I don't want to live in a slum for our first couple of years— like other newly-weds.

Brindsley Shhh! Shhhh!

Carol What's the matter with you?

Brindsley The gods listen, darling. They've given me a terrible night so far. They may do worse.

Carol (*cooing*) I know, darling. You've had a filthy evening. Poor baby. But I'll fight them with you. I don't care a fig for those naughty old gods. (*She looks up*) Do you hear? Not a single little figipoo!

Clea aims at the voice and sends a jet of vodka splashing down over Carol

Ahh!!!

Brindsley What is it?

Carol It's raining!

Brindsley Don't be stupid.

Carol I'm all wet!

Brindsley How can you be?

Clea throws vodka over a wider area. Harold gets it

Harold Hey, what's going on?

Brindsley What?

Colonel What are you hollerin' for?

He gets a slug of vodka in the face

Ahh!

Brindsley (*inspired*) It's a leak—the water mains must have gone now!

Harold Oh, good God!

Brindsley It must be!

Mischievously, Clea raps her bottle loudly on the top stair. There is a terrified silence. All look up. Pause

Harold Don't say there's someone else here.

Brindsley Good Lord!

Colonel Who's there?

Silence from above

Come on! I know you're there!

Pause

Brindsley (*improvising wildly*) I—I bet you it's Mrs Punnet.

Clea looks astonished

Colonel Who?
Brindsley (*for Clea's benefit*) Mrs Punnet. My cleaning woman. She
comes here every Friday.
Carol But what would she be doing here *now*?
Brindsley I—I've just remembered! I mentioned to her yesterday I was
giving a party tonight and she said she'd look in and tidy up the place
for me!
Colonel But dammit man, it's ten o'clock!
Harold She can't be that conscientious! Not from what you've told me.
Brindsley Oh, but she is! You haven't met her—you can't *imagine* how
devoted she is...! One night she turned up at *midnight*, and told me she
couldn't sleep for thinking how dirty the place might be!
Colonel But when did she come?
Brindsley She probably just slipped in and upstairs without our hearing.
She's very discreet. She actually wears special swansdown slippers to
keep noise to the minimum.
Colonel Well, let's just see if it's her, shall we?
Brindsley Oh no, sir—she hates being disturbed!
Colonel (*calling*) Mrs Punnet...! Is that you...? (*Louder*) Mrs Punnet!!!

Pause

Clea (*deliberately deciding on an old Cockney voice*) 'Allo! Yes?
Brindsley (*weakly*) It is. Good heavens, Mrs Punnet, what on earth are
you doing up there?
Clea I'm just giving your bedroom a bit of a tidy, sir.
Brindsley At this time of night?

The mischief in Clea begins to take over

Clea I'm afraid I was delayed, but better late than never, sir, as they say.
I know how you like your bedroom to be nice and inviting when you're
giving one of your parties.
Colonel When did you come, madam?
Clea Just a few minutes ago, sir. I didn't like to disturb you, so I came on

up 'ere. But I can't seem to find the light. It's as dark as Newgate's
Knocker... Are you playing one of your kinky games, Mr Miller?
Brindsley No, Mrs Punnet. We've had a fuse. It's all over the house.
Clea Oh, a fuse! I thought it might be one of your kinky games in the dark,
sir. Perhaps the one with the rubber underclothes and those little whips.
(*She starts to come downstairs*)
Brindsley (*distinctly*) It is a fuse, Mrs Punnet. The man is mending it now.
The lights will be on *any minute!*
Clea Well, that'll be a relief for you, won't it? (*She dashes the vodka
accurately in his face, passes him by, and comes into the room*)
Brindsley Yes, of course. Now why don't you just go on home now?
There's nothing you can do here tonight.
Clea Are you sure of that, sir?

*During the following, Brindsley gropes around the room frantically to
find her, but she eludes him*

Brindsley Well not with this fuse—it's pointless, isn't it?
Clea Oh no, sir! I could clean this place with my eyes shut. And I'd like
to—really! I'd hate your guests to see it as it usually is. Bras and panties
in the sink—contraceptives on the floor—and marriage—uana seeds
simply *everywhere!*

*Brindsley muzzles her with his hand. She bites it hard, and he drops to his
knees in silent agony*

Colonel Please watch what you say, madam. You don't know it, but
you're in the presence of Mr Miller's fiancée.
Clea Fiancée?
Colonel Yes, and I am her father.
Clea Well, I never...! Oh, Mr Miller! I'm so 'appy for you...! Fiancée!
Oh, sir. And you never *told* me!
Brindsley I was keeping it a surprise.
Clea Well, I never! Oh, how lovely...! May I kiss you, sir, please?
Brindsley (*on his knees*) Well, yes, yes, of course...

Clea gropes for his ear, finds it, and twists it

Clea Oh, sir, I'm so pleased for you! And for *you*, miss, too!

Carol Thank you.
Clea (*to Colonel*) And for *you*, sir.
Colonel Thank you.
Clea (*wickedly*) You must be—Miss Clea's father!
Colonel Miss Clea? I don't understand.

Triumphantly, Clea sticks out her tongue at Brindsley, who collapses his length on the floor, face down, in a gesture of total surrender. For him it is the end. The evening can hold no further disasters for him

Clea (*to Carol*) Well, I never! So you've got him at last! Well done, Miss Clea! I never thought you would—not after four years...
Brindsley No—no—no—no...!
Clea Forgive me, sir, if I'm speaking out of turn, but you must admit you take a long time proposing. Four years is a long time to be courting one woman.
Brindsley (*weakly*) Mrs Punnet, *please!*
Carol Four years?
Clea Well, yes, dear. It's been all of that and a bit more, hasn't it? (*In a stage whisper*) And of course it's just in time really, isn't it? It was getting a bit prominent, your little bun in the oven.

Carol screeches with disgust. Brindsley covers his ears

Oh, Miss, I don't mean that's why he popped the question. Of course it's not. He's always been stuck on you. He told me so, not one week ago, in this room. (*Sentimentally*) "Mrs Punnet," he says, "Mrs Punnet, as far as I'm concerned you can keep the rest of them—Miss Clea will always be on the top of the heap for me." "Oh," I says, "then what about that débutante bit, Carol, the one you're always telling me about? That Colonel's daughter." "Oh, er," he says, "she's just a bit of Knightsbridge candy floss. A couple of licks and you've 'ad 'er."

There is a long pause. Clea is now sitting on the table, swinging her vodka bottle in absolute command

Colonel (*at last grappling with the situation; faintly*) Did you say four years, madam?
Clea (*in her own voice, quietly*) Yes, Colonel. Four years, in this room.
Harold I know that voice. It's Clea!
Carol (*horrified*) Clea!

Brindsley (*unconvincingly*) Clea?
Colonel I don't understand anything that's going on in this room!
Clea I know. It is a very odd room, isn't it? It's like a magic dark room, where everything happens the wrong way round. Rain falls indoors, the daily comes at night, and turns in a second from a nice maid into a nasty mistress.
Brindsley Shut up, for God's sake!
Clea At last! One real word of protest! Have you finished lying, then? Have you eaten the last crumb of humble pie? Oh, you coward, *you bloody coward!* Just because you didn't want to marry me, did you have to settle for this lot?
Carol Marry!
Colonel Marry?
Clea Four years of meaning to end in this triviality! Miss Laughingly-Known-As and her Daddypoo!
Carol Stop her, for God's sake!
Colonel And how would you suggest I did that?
Carol Well, where's all that bloody resource you keep talking about?

The Colonel goes to her but takes Clea's hand by mistake

Colonel Now calm down, Dumpling. Keep your head... There—hold my hand, that's it. Now Daddy's here. Everything is under control. All right?
Clea Are you sure that is your daughter's hand you're holding, Colonel?
Colonel What? Carol, isn't this your hand?
Carol No.
Clea You must have lived with your daughter for well over twenty years, Colonel. What remarkable use you've made of your eyes.

There is another pause. The Colonel moves away in embarrassment

(*Wickedly*) All right! *My* kinky game time...! Let's all play Guess the Hand.
Harold Oh, good God!
Clea Or would you rather play Guess the Teeth, Harold? Who's got teeth like a picket fence?
Carol How disgusting!
Clea Well, that's me, dear. (*Carol's accent*) I'm Queen Disgustipoo! (*She seizes Carol's hand and puts it into Harold's*) All right—*who's that?*

Carol I don't know.

Clea Guess.

Carol I don't know, and I don't care.

Clea Oh, go on. Have a go!

Carol It's Brin, of course: you can't trick me like that! It's Brindsley's stupid hand.

Harold I'm afraid you're wrong. It's me.

Carol (*struggling*) It's not. You're lying.

Harold (*holding on*) I'm not. I don't lie.

Carol You're lying...! You're lying!

Harold I'm not.

Carol breaks away and blunders up stage. She is becoming hysterical

Clea You try it, Harold.

Harold I'm not playing. It's a bloody silly game.

Clea Go on... (*She seizes his hand and puts it into Brindsley's*) Well?

Harold It's Brin.

Brindsley Yes.

Clea Well done! (*She sits on the low stool*)

Carol (*outraged*) How does he know that? How does *he* know your hand and I don't?

Brindsley Calm down, Carol.

Carol Answer me! I want to know!

Brindsley Stop it!

Carol I won't!

Brindsley You're getting hysterical!

Carol Leave me alone! I want to go home.

And suddenly Miss Furnival gives a short scream and blunders out through the curtains. She is dishevelled and evidently out of control in a world of her own released by drink

All freeze

Miss Furnival (*rapidly and clearly*) Carts—carts—shopping carts in the supermarket...! All those wire carts filled with babies and bottles! They aim at you on purpose...! No help from anyone. People used to say "Yes, Madam. Thank you, Madam! Do you want it delivered?" Now all they say is "Cornflakes over there", and leave you to yourself! "Biscuits over there—Brillo over there—cat food over there!" Pink stamps, green stamps, free balloons, television dinners! *Oh Daddy, it's awful!* And then the godless ones—all those heathens in helmets, laughing me to scorn...! But not for long. Oh no! Who shall stand when *He* appeareth? *He'll* stop them. He'll strike them from their motorcycles! He'll dash their helmets to the ground. Verily I say—there shall be an end to sneering! An end to sniggering in leather...! Keep off me...! Keep off...! Keep off...! Keep off...! Keep off! (*She runs hysterically across the room and collides with Harold*)

Harold holds Miss Furnival

Harold (*gently*) Come on, Ferny. I think it's time we went home.
Miss Furnival Yes. You're quite right. (*With an attempt at grandeur*) I'm sorry I can't stay any longer, Mr Miller: but your millionaire is unpardonably late. So typical of modern manners... Express my regrets, if you please.
Brindsley Certainly.

Leaning heavily on Harold's arm, Miss Furnival leaves the room

(*Shutting the door after them*) Thank you, Clea. Thank you very much.
Clea Any time.
Brindsley You had no right.
Clea No?
Brindsley *You* walked out on *me.*

He joins her on the low stool. During the following dialogue, the Colonel and Carol stand frozen with astonished anger

Clea Is that what I did?
Brindsley You said you never wanted to see me again.
Clea I never saw you at all—how could you be walked out on? You should *live* in the dark, Brindsley. It's your natural element.
Brindsley Whatever that means.
Clea It means you don't really want to be seen. Why is that, Brindsley? Do you think if someone really saw you, they would never love you?
Brindsley Oh, go away!

Clea I want to know.

Brindsley Yes, you always want to know. Pick-pick-pick away! Why is *that*, Clea? Have you ever thought why you need to do that? Well?

Clea Perhaps because I care about you.

Brindsley Perhaps there's nothing to care about. Just a fake artist.

Clea Stop pitying yourself. It's always your vice. I told you when I met you: you could either be a good artist, or a chic fake. You didn't like it, because I refused just to give you applause.

Brindsley God knows, you certainly did that!

Clea Is that what *she* gives you? Twenty hours of ego-massage every day?

Brindsley At least our life together isn't a replica of the Holy Inquisition. I didn't have an affair with you: it was just four years of nooky with Torquemada!

Clea And don't say you didn't enjoy it!

Brindsley Enjoy it? I hated every second of it.

Clea Yes, I remember.

Brindsley Every second!

Clea I recall.

Brindsley When you left for Finland, it was the happiest day of my life.

Clea Mine, too!

Brindsley I sighed with relief!

Clea So did I!

Brindsley I went out dancing that very night!

Clea So did I. It was out with the lyre and the timbrel!

Brindsley Good. Then that's all right.

Clea Fine.

Brindsley Super!

Clea Duper!

Brindsley It's lovely to see you looking so happy.

Clea You too. Radiant with self-fulfilment.

A pause. Suddenly they both giggle. She falls happily against his shoulder

Colonel (*very angry*) No doubt this is very funny to you two.

Clea It is, quite, actually.

Colonel I'm not so easily amused, however, madam.

Brindsley Now look, Colonel——

Colonel Hold your tongue, sir, I'm talking. Do you know what would have happened to a young man in my day who dared to treat a girl the way you have treated my Dumpling?

Brindsley Well, I assume, Colonel——
Colonel Hold your tongue, I'm talking!
Carol Oh, leave it, Daddy. Let's just go home.
Colonel In a moment, Dumpling. Kindly leave this to me.
Brindsley Look, Carol, I can explain——
Carol (*raging*) What the hell's to explain? All the time you were going
with me, *she* was in the background—that's all there is to it. What were
you doing? Weighing us up...? Here! (*She pulls off her engagement
ring*)
Brindsley What?
Carol Your ring. Take the bloody thing back! (*She throws it*)

The ring hits the Colonel in the eye

Colonel My eye! My damned eye!

Clea starts to laugh again

(*In a mounting fury, clutching his eye*) Oh, very droll, madam! Very
droll indeed! Laugh your fill...! Miller! I asked you a question. Do you
know what would have happened to a young lout like you in my day?
Brindsley Happened, sir?
Colonel (*quietly*) You'd have been thrashed, sir.
Brindsley (*nervously*) Thrashed——

*The man of war begins to go after him, feeling his way in the dark, like
some furious robot*

Colonel You'd have felt the mark of a father's horsewhip across your
seducer's shoulders.
Brindsley (*retreating before the Colonel's groping advance*) Would I,
sir?
Colonel You'd have raised your guttersnipe voice in a piteous scream for
mercy and forgiveness!!

*A terrible scream is indeed heard from the hall. They freeze, listening as
it comes nearer and nearer*

*The door is flung open and Harold plunges into the room. He is wild-
eyed with rage: a lit and bent taper shakes in his furious hand*

The stage darkens

Harold Ooooooh! You villain!
Brindsley Harold——
Harold You skunky, conniving little villain!
Brindsley What's the matter?
Harold (*raging*) Have you seen the state of my room? My room—my
   lovely room—the most elegant and cared for in the entire district? One
   chair turned absolutely upside down! One chair on top of another like
   a Portobello junk shop! And that's not all, is it Brindsley? Oh no—that's
   not the worst by a long chalk!
Brindsley Long chalk?
Harold Don't play the innocent with me. I thought I had a friend living
   here all these years. I didn't know I was living opposite a stinking little
   thief!
Brindsley Harold!
Harold (*hysterical*) This is my reward, isn't it? After years of looking
   after you—because you're too much of a slob to do it for yourself—to
   have my best pieces stolen from me to impress your new girlfriend, and
   her daddy! *Where's my sofa?* My irreplaceable *chaise-longue*?
Brindsley (*unhappily*) Behind the curtain.
Harold Unbelievable.
Brindsley It was an emergency, Harold——
Harold Don't speak another word. You and that little nit can carry it back
   to my room right now. And any other bits you've taken. (*Loftily*) This
   is the end of our relationship, Brindsley. I doubt if we shall be speaking
   again! (*Drawing himself up with all the offended dignity of which he is
   capable, he twitches his raincoat off the table. Inside it, of course, is the
   Buddha, which falls out of it on to the floor and smashes beyond repair*)

There is a terrible silence. Pause

   (*With the quietness of the near-crazy*) I think I'm going to have to smash
   you, Brindsley.
Brindsley (*nervously*) Now steady on, Harold ... don't be rash...
Harold Oh, yes, I'm very much afraid I'll have to smash *you*... Smash
   for smash—that's fair do's. (*He pulls one of the long metal prongs out
   of the sculpture*) Smash for smash. Smash for *smash*! (*Terrifyingly, he
   advances on Brindsley, holding the prong like a sword, the taper
   burning in his other hand*)

Brindsley (*retreating*) Stop it, Harold. You've gone mad!
Colonel Well done, sir. I think it's time for the reckoning.

The Colonel grabs the other prong and also advances

Brindsley (*retreating from them both*) Now just a minute, Colonel. Be
   reasonable...! Let's not revert to savages...! Harold, I appeal to you—
   you've always had civilized instincts! Don't join the Army...!
Carol (*grimly advancing also*) Get him, Daddy! Get him! Get him!
Brindsley (*horrified at her*) Carol!
Carol (*malevolently*) Get him! Get him! Get——
Brindsley (*in appeal*) Clea!

Clea leaps up and blows out the taper. Lights up

Colonel Dammit!

Clea grabs Brindsley's hand and pulls him out of danger

Harold (*to Carol*) Hush up, Colonel. We'll be able to hear them
   breathing.
Colonel Good idea! S.T. Smart Tactics, sir!

*Silence. They listen. Brindsley climbs carefully on to the table and silently
pulls Clea up after him. Harold and the Colonel, prodding and slashing
the darkness with their swords, grimly hunt their quarry. Twenty seconds
pass*

Suddenly, with a bang, Schuppanzigh opens the trap from below

Both men turn and advance on it warily

The electrician disappears again below

*They have almost reached it, on tiptoe, when there is another crash—this
time from the hall. Someone has again tripped over the milk bottles.
Harold and the Colonel immediately swing round and start stalking up
stage, still on tiptoe*

George Bamberger enters. He is quite evidently a millionaire. Dressed in the Gulbenkian manner, he wears a beard, an eyeglass, a frock coat, a top hat, and an orchid. He carries a large deaf aid. Bewildered, he advances into the room

Stealthily, the two armed men stalk him up stage as he silently gropes his way down stage and passes between them. Bamberger speaks in a middle-aged German voice, as near to the voice of Schuppanzigh as possible

Bamberger 'Allo, please! Mr Miller?

Harold and the Colonel spin round in a third direction

Harold Oh, it's the electrician!
Bamberger 'Allo, please?
Colonel What the devil are you doing up here?

Schuppanzigh appears at the trap

Have you mended the fuse?
Harold Or are you going to keep us in the dark all night?
Schuppanzigh Don't worry. The fuse is mended. (*He comes out of the trap*)

Bamberger goes round the stage, right

Harold Thank God for that.
Bamberger (*still groping around*) Hallo, please? Mr Miller—vere ar you? Vy zis darkness? Is a joke, yes?
Schuppanzigh (*incensed*) Ah, no! That is not very funny, good people— just because I am a foreigner, to imitate my voice. You English can be the rudest people on earth!
Bamberger (*imperiously*) Mr Miller! I have come here to give attention to your sculptures!
Schuppanzigh *Gott in Himmel!*
Bamberger *Gott in Himmel!*
Brindsley God, it's him! *Bamberger!*
Harold Bamberger!
Colonel Bamberger!

They freeze. The millionaire sets off, left, toward the open trap

Brindsley Don't worry, Mr Bamberger. We've had a fuse, but it's mended now.

Bamberger (*irritably*) Mr Miller!

Clea You'll have to speak up. He's deaf.

Brindsley (*shouting*) Don't worry, Mr Bamberger! We've had a fuse, but it's all right now...! (*Standing on the table, he clasps Clea happily*)

Bamberger misses the trap by inches

Oh, Clea, that's true. Everything's all right now! Just in the nick of time!

But as Brindsley says this, Bamberger turns and falls into the open trapdoor. Schuppanzigh slams it shut with his foot

Schuppanzigh So! Here's now an end to your troubles! Like Jehovah in the Sacred Testament, I give you the most miraculous gift of the Creation! Light!

Clea Light!

Brindsley Oh, thank God. *Thank God!*

Schuppanzigh goes to the switch

Harold (*grimly*) I wouldn't thank Him too soon, Brindsley, if I were you!

Colonel Nor would I, Brindsley, if I were you!

Carol Nor would I, Brinny-Poo, if I were you!

Schuppanzigh (*grandly*) Then thank *me*! For I shall play God for this second! (*He claps his hands*) Attend all of you. God said: "Let there be light!" And there *was*, good people, suddenly—astoundingly—instantaneously—inconceivably—inexhaustibly—inextinguishably and eternally—*light*! (*With a great flourish, he flicks the light switch*)

Instant darkness. The turntable of the record player starts up again, and with an exultant crash the Sousa march falls on the audience—and blazes away in the black

Curtain

FURNITURE AND PROPERTY LIST

Further dressing may be added at the director's discretion

On stage: Doormat. *Under it:* key
Curtain
Metal sculptures
Mobiles
Manikins
Toys
Bric-à-brac
3 elegant Regency chairs in gold leaf
Regency *chaise-longue*
Small Queen Anne table. *On it:* a fine opaline lamp with a silk
    shade, good Coalport vase containing summer flowers
Cheap square table. *On it:* drinks
Cheap round table. *On it:* cloth, Wedgwood bowl
Low stool. *On it:* fine porcelain Buddha
Record player
Bizarre iron sculpture dominated by two long detachable metal
    prongs, and hung with metal pieces
Non-figurative paintings
Glasses
Soda syphon
Light switch
Telephone
Packing case
Bed

Off stage: Milk bottles
Smart raincoat, small weekend bag with handles (**Harold**)
Poor, broken-down chair (**Brindsley**)
Old rocking-chair (**Brindsley**)
Cheap old chair (**Brindsley**)
Flight bag (**Clea**)
Large toolbag, bearing London Electricity Board label
    (**Schuppanzigh**)
Plastic toothmug (**Clea**)
Lit and bent taper (**Harold**)

Personal: **Colonel:** lighter
Harold: matches
Clea: dark glasses
Schuppanzigh: torch
Carol: engagement ring
Bamberger: eyeglass, orchid, large deaf aid

LIGHTING PLOT

Property fittings required : table lamp
1 interior. The same throughout

To open: Complete darkness

Cue 1   Sousa march stops   (Page 5)
                   Brilliant light floods the stage

Cue 2   **Colonel** enters with a lighter   (Page 11)
                   Lights down a little

Cue 3   **Colonel** goes off into the studio   (Page 12)
                   Lights up to full

Cue 4   **Colonel** enters   (Page 13)
                   Lights down a little

Cue 5   **Colonel** snaps off his lighter   (Page 13)
                   Lights up to full

Cue 6   **Colonel** lights his lighter   (Page 14)
                   Lights down a little

Cue 7   **Colonel** snaps off his lighter   (Page 15)
                   Lights up to full

Cue 8   **Colonel** lights the lighter after several tries   (Page 16)
                   Lights up and down correspondingly

Cue 9   **Brindsley** blows out the lighter   (Page 17)
                   Lights up to full

Cue 10   **Harold** strikes a match   (Page 17)
                   Lights down a little

Cue 11   **Brindsley** blows out the match   (Page 17)
                   Lights up to full

EFFECTS PLOT

Cue 1   **Brindsley**: "Amen."   (Page 5)
           Loud Sousa march starts and immediately runs down

Cue 2   **Brindsley**: "Damn, damn, damn, damn, damn, damn!"   (Page 6)
           Telephone rings

Cue 3   **Schuppanzigh** switches on light   (Page 57)
           Sousa march starts with exultant crash and blazes on